REFLECTIONS OF A COLORED GIRL

About the Audio Essay Series "Reflections of a Colored Girl" on WGCU PBS & NPR for Southwest Florida

"August 8, 2023

'In my life, I have found myself as a colored, a negro, a Black, an African American, and a person of color. This is my reflection as a colored girl.' This phrase opens each essay heard on WGCU FM from Martha R. Bireda, Ph.D. Dr. Bireda is a writer, lecturer, and living history performer with over 30 years of experience as a lecturer, consultant and trainer for issues related to race, class, and gender, working with educators, law enforcement, and business, and civic leaders. Bireda also is the Director of the Blanchard House Museum of African American History and Culture of Charlotte County, located in Punta Gorda, Florida. The audio series, "Reflections of a Colored Girl," will be featured weekly on WGCU FM for the next five months. This is the first."

In Spring 2024, "Reflections of a Colored Girl" the Documentary will be airing on WGCU PBS & NPR for Southwest Florida

REFLECTIONS OF A COLORED GIRL

By Martha R. Bireda

Blue Ocean Press

Copyright @ 2024 Blue Ocean Press

All Rights Reserved.

This publication may not be reproduced, stored in a retrieval system or transmitted in any form or by any means, electronic, mechanical, photocopying, recording, or otherwise, without prior written permission of the publisher, except by a reviewer who may quote brief passages in a review to be printed in a periodical.

Published by:
Blue Ocean Press

U.S. Office
P.O. Box 510818
Punta Gorda, Florida 33950

Japan Office
6F & 7F TOC Daiichi Bldg.
1-8-3 Shibuya
Shibuya-ku, Tokyo, Japan 150-0002

URL: http://www.blueoceanpublications.com
Email: books@blueoceanpublications.com

ISBN: 978-4-902837-44-5

Table of Contents

May 2, 2022	7
Preface	11
May 2, 1945	17
The Holler	23
Nigger	29
My Hero	35
Coming Home	45
Traveling While Colored	55
The Reality of Being "Colored"	61
The Value of Education	67
The Back of the Bus – Education	73
Empowering Lessons for a Colored Girl	79
The Road Ahead	85
Granny	91
Mommy	97
negro or Negro	109
Culturally Deprived	115
The Essayist	123
Redefining My Identity	131
What Does it Mean to Be American	139
Education	145
Person of the Global Majority	153
Conclusion	161
Acknowledgements	165

May 2, 2022

The seventy-fifth birthday is referred to as a "milestone birthday". One has lived three-quarters of a century. My "diamond jubilee" was marred however by several events. First, we were deep into the COVID 19 pandemic: a time of physical isolation, protecting oneself and others possibly from the virus, not a time for a celebration of family and friends. It was a time of great uncertainty and fear.

Some twenty-three days later, on May 25, 2020, George Floyd's killing by a policeman altered American society. A real racial reckoning had begun which included protests not only across America but the global society as well.

These events initiated my life review, as described by Erik Erickson which would lead me to understand and evaluate my life in terms of "Ego Integrity or Despair. This life review has brought me to writing this memoir.

As I contemplated the accomplishments and successes of my life, I have had a good life. I have earned four degrees, owned my own consulting business, loved my work, traveled to much of the world, and have two very successful adult children.

On September 28, 2022, my little town of Punta Gorda was the center of the eye of Hurricane Ian, which changed all of our lives, including mine, to a great degree. The museum of which I am director needs extensive work to be repaired, I am writing this from my hotel room as my home suffered extensive damage as well. This space, like that which came with the pandemic is giving me an opportunity to continue my life review, to look deeply into my past, to explore the beliefs and values of whom I am today.

My life began as a colored girl, born in a tiny room reserved for "coloreds" at a hospital in Arcadia, Florida, a short distance from my mother's home in Punta Gorda. That tiny room was symbolic of the constricted life that was supposed to be mine because of the "C" on my birth certificate. My cousin named me "May Queen", however the larger society into which I was born would see me very differently. I was to grow and live a life as a second-class citizen, one of inequality in every aspect of my life.

As I review my first sixteen years of life growing up in a Jim Crow system, I realize my accomplishments and successes are the result of beliefs, values, and expectations learned as a "colored girl". This book being written as I sit in a hotel room, living in the "space" provided by nature this time, is a collection of those experiences and lessons. While I learned these specific lessons because of my supposed place in America's racial hierarchy, they are human lessons that can serve to empower any and all who believe they are more valuable and worthy than others believe them to be.

Preface

Image of Zora Neale Hurston, Public Domain

"I am not tragically colored. There is no great sorrow dammed up in my soul, nor lurking behind my eyes. I do not mind at all. I do not belong to the sobbing school of Negrohood who hold that nature somehow has given them a lowdown dirty deal and those feelings are all hurt about it. Even in the helter-skelter skirmish that is my life, I have seen that the world is to the strong regardless of a little pigmentation more or less. No, I do not weep at the world, I am too busy sharpening my oyster knife."
- Zora Neale Hurston

Zora Neale Hurston is one of my favorite authors and it is her philosophy about race, being "colored" which I believe and adhere. There have been many books written about the horrors of being "colored" especially during the Jim Crow era, and the feelings and pain that one cannot escape. Little has been written about the agency of the colored to not only survive but to thrive despite the barriers they encountered.

Reflections of a Colored Girl will offer a significantly different narrative, one that yes describes the segregation and discrimination this colored girl experienced, but more importantly, the beliefs, values, and actions of my family, school, and community that inspired, challenged, and expected me to be the human being that I became. Like Zora, "I am not tragically colored."

I am not the only "colored" child of my generation that was empowered during this period, many more can relate the same story. It was during this period, that the colored developed exceptional institutions of learning, created great works of art and music, and created over 200 vibrant and successful colored business districts. Tulsa and Durham are just two of these monumental accomplishments despite the forces working against them.

It is during the Jim Crow era that the mythology of white superiority and black inferiority was solidly refuted. Colored people excelled without the paternalism of whites, without legal rights being given, or the moral convictions of white Americans changing. We colored used our spiritual power to understand, and African traditions to rise above the psychological needs of white America to dehumanize and control our lives. We are not and have never been the stereotypical image in the conditioned white mind.

W.E.B. Du Bois refers to the existence of a barrier prohibiting genuine understanding and equality between black and white people as the "veil". It is my intention in these essays to lift the "veil" and reveal the authentic identities of those of my generation who were designated as "colored". I believe that sharing true and accurate history can heal. I offer these essays as a vehicle to foster racial healing.

You might be surprised as you read the essays in this book. They will possibly seem to be unreal, impossible, however, these essays reflect the life and the consciousness of one labeled at birth and who grew up as a "colored" girl. This is my life story from birth to now 78 years old. I have accepted and grown from every aspect of my life; I feel a sense of coherence and wholeness. I thank every family member, teacher, and resident of the village who loved, shaped and created the conditions for my self-empowerment as a "colored girl" during my formative years. These essays are dedicated to you.

Martha Russell Bireda

May 2, 1945

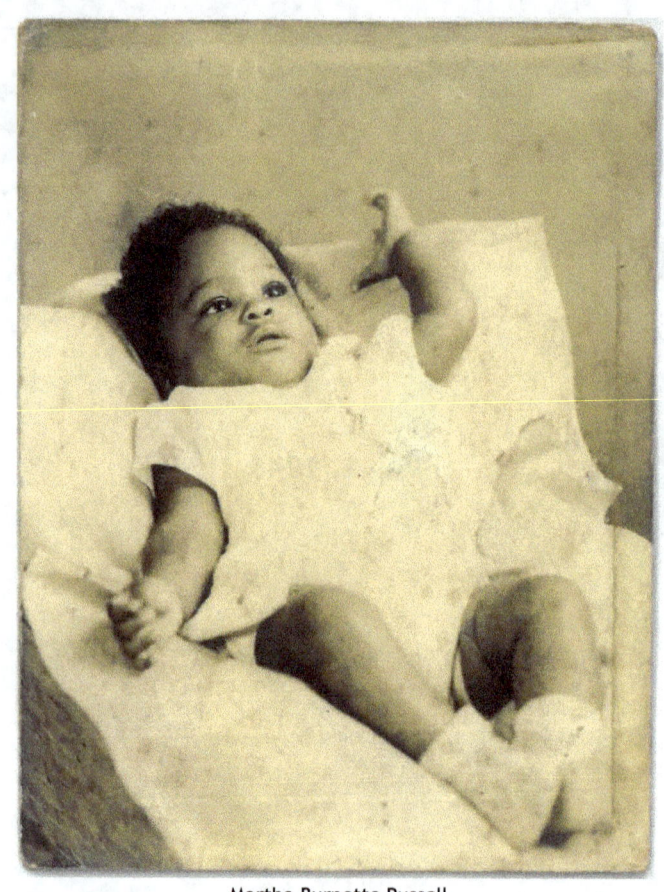

Martha Burnette Russell

Bernice and Martha

I was born on May 2, 1945, in the colored section of Arcadia General Hospital, in a Florida town originally established to be all-white and Christian. The tiny room in which I was born, reserved for "coloreds" was symbolic of the circumscribed life planned for me. I was born into a society that would not recognize my beauty, my intelligence, or my humanity. But I was welcomed with all the love my 21-year-old mother and 26-year-old father and extended family could possibly give. I was the first-born on both sides of the family, and all of my life would hold the special honor that affords. I would also be the only child of my parents as my mother's congenital heart defect meant she would bear no more children. I came with a head of curly hair, eyes so dark they appeared black, and *cafe con leche* complexion. My maternal grandmother named me "Mamma Sweet" and an older cousin accorded me the title of May Queen. Those messages of love so sweetly and persistently given built the spirit of this colored girl.

What did it mean to be born colored in 1945?

The life meant for a colored girl born during the Jim Crow era (1877-1964) would not be that of royalty but of restriction in every aspect of my life: as a "colored," I would be a victim of the "veil", the term coined by W.E.B. Du Bois which indicated erroneous beliefs based on a mythology of black intellectual, cultural, and moral inferiority: I would attend poorly financed and equipped schools designed to be inferior to those of white students, and my teachers would be paid less than their white counterparts.

Jim Crow laws would require me to experience segregated seating, eating, sleeping, restrooms, waiting rooms, ticket windows when traveling. I would be denied entrance to public libraries, parks, swimming pools and playgrounds. The racial hierarchy would attempt to condemn me to employment in a menial job that required my subservience. Jim Crow custom and etiquette would expect my manners, voice, attitude and demeaner to enforce the mythology of white superiority. Most critically, white socialization would require that I know and keep my place in the racial hierarchy.

Perhaps along the journey of these 78 years I have been scarred by ugly names, Jim Crow rules and outright fear of those who surrounded me, but were not my own. I know that the strength and love of the brown hands who first held me created a spirit within me that made me not only proud of being colored, but even established within me a sense of empowerment.

I do not see myself as a victim. I have a life that I love, but I am a realist. I understand that education, degrees, and a certain status separate me only marginally from the stereotypical and negative images of those less fortunate than myself. Only when all my people are free from the distorted images that continue to bind them will I be totally free.

The "Holler"

Aunt Rosa and Uncle James Russell
The Holler

The Holler

Are there spaces where humanity rather than one's color prevails? Where one's interdependence outweighs the socially constructed labels meant to divide? The holler was that place. The holler was where I spent the first six years of my life. My father soon to be a veteran of WWII was never informed or considered to receive the GI educational or housing benefits to which he was entitled. After my birth, we returned to his home, and settled in the "holler" of Marion, a small town in Southwestern Virginia, in a house built in the 1920s by his uncle.

The holler, as we knew it, was the valley that lay at the bottom of a steep hill. In the holler lived the Russell's and three white families, the Coleys, the Kirkos, and Roy Bee. Sarah and Will Coley lived next door to my grandmother, Lelia Russell, and across the road from my Aunt Rosa and Uncle James. Mrs. Kirko, a widow, lived across the road from my home. At the top of the hill in a very weathered house, lived Roy Bee, a white who worked for my uncle.

One reached the holler by following a one lane road, the apex of which required drivers to stop and blow the horn to alert an approaching car. On the left of the steep curve, lay the land of the Russell's, my ancestors. It stretched from the top of the hill to the creek below. Flowers and plants flowed down the hill. At the bottom lay an oval race track, the center of which was planted with tobacco. It was on this track that horses were trained for show. My uncle's unpainted, weathered house sat back from the road next to the smoke house. The outhouse stood next to a little shack that served as my uncle's man cave. A rock path took one down past the oval track, the center filled with tobacco plants, where horses were ridden and tamed, a pig pen, a creek and the spring which was the source of drinking water. The house in which I lived sat high above the creek.

Sarah and Will Coley, the newest residents, lived in the most modern house with a well, modern appliances and a telephone; the telephone of which my grandmother Lelia and Aunt Rosa, had liberal use. They were simply neighbors, all on a first-name basis, there was no going into the back door, no subservience. My grandmother Lelia lived in a white frame house with green trim and a porch on which there were two swings. One had to climb steps made from large stones to reach the porch. What I remember most about the house was the kitchen with the coal and wood-burning stove that spanned the length of the house. Outside was an outhouse and a large, terraced garden that climbed the hill.

The folks who lived in the holler exchanged meats and vegetables. The Coley's had cows and my uncle pigs. The cardinal rule of coloreds and whites eating and drinking together was broken every weekend. Whites gathered with my uncle and his brothers on that day to drink moonshine or bourbon underneath my uncle's house. They sat for hours drinking, telling jokes and lies.

Beyond the steep curve in town, blacks and whites were separated from each other by a wall in the Broad

Street Tearoom, an establishment owned by Mr. Sharp, a black man. Blacks and whites could peer into each other's space, but could not legally drink together. In the holler those laws were broken.

We were in our way an interdependent, self-contained community, not so much defined by race, but by our being "country" rather than town dwellers. As folks in the holler, colored and whites, climbed and rounded the steep curve, the specter of race entered their lives. The whites became "white" but not in the same way as those who lived in antebellum mansions along Highway 11 or in the solidly middle and upper class Wassona Park. My father and uncles became "colored" with all the conventions of Jim Crow. I am sure that my father and uncles, as well as our white neighbors, breathed a sigh of relief when they rounded that steep curve that brought them home to the holler. There they became simply human.

In those early years of my life, I only saw relationships and friendships between neighbors. The color of their skins had little meaning as there was a parade of different skin colors in my own family from light, bright, and almost white to light and dark browns.

"Nigger"

Carnegie High School

My lesson in being colored began in earnest when we rounded the steep curve from the holler and moved into town when I was seven so that I could attend school. The first time I heard or remember being called "nigger" was by two white boys passing my house on Franklin Street. I intuitively knew that that name made me the "other".

In Marion, we lived in a racially mixed neighborhood, my neighbors across the street and to the right and left of my house were white. Betty Repass who lived in a large two-story rooming house across from our house was one of my babysitters. The other was Bobbi Louise, a colored girl who lived with her family in a two-story brick home on a huge lot on which the colored kids in the neighborhood often played softball. In all, eleven colored families lived in my neighborhood. Relationships were cordial but the rules and customs of Jim Crow were understood. I sometimes played with the two white girls across the street, but we never entered each other's houses. By and large, we lived separate colored and white lives in the same neighborhood.

I definitely understood the power of being white when it was time to enter school. The colored kids had to walk at least two to three miles to school. Up the hill to and across main street then up another hill, through Iron Street, a colored section to Carnegie High School. Carnegie was a brick school built during the Rosenwald era. Miss Thompson taught grades 1-3 in one room, Miss Campbell 4-6 across the hall, Miss Ellis 7-9 at the other end of the hall, and "Fess"

Dabney (short for professor) taught grades 9-10 and was the principal. Students graduated from Carnegie and were able to attend college after completing 11th grade. There was a large auditorium in which Friday chapel as well as spectacular dramatic and musical programs created by Miss Thompson, also the music teacher was responsible. The cafeteria was in the basement and bathrooms outside.

Attending Carnegie was the typical experience for colored children. Overcrowded classrooms, not enough textbooks, old textbooks, no lab equipment, and no library. Our educational resources, materials and our structure were definitely separate and unequal.

Next to Carnegie, was the colored pool, which Miss Thompson opened and operated in the summer. There is a very famous state park, Hungry Mother State Park located in Marion, that colored were prohibited from using. Here there was everything from horseback riding, to boating, swimming, and picnicking. We colored had to drive 25 miles to a public picnic area for colored only.

Jim Crow was pervasive in Marion. We colored understood and felt its weight. Aside from separate schools were separate sections of the theater, colored sat in the balcony, separate eras for colored at the drive-in, no admittance to dining establishments or hotels, and standing at the counter to purchase an ice cream cone.

It was an interesting separation, integrated neighborhoods, but none but the least social interaction. There was no predominately colored neighborhood, cultural and social relationships were related to benevolent societies and two churches. The largest colored church, Mt. Pleasant Methodist was not located in a colored neighborhood but in a white area in the southern end of town.

It became clear to me when we moved to town that my life as a colored girl would be different, that I was and would be treated like the other. "Nigger", a name I never heard in the holler was a constant refrain in town. It was in town, however, that I learned my most important lesson about self-empowerment from my very own father.

My Hero

Bernice and Alonzo Russell

Martha, Jaha, Alonzo

Russell Hall
Blue Ridge Job Corps
Marion, Virginia

Russell Hall

My father, Alonzo Clifton Russell (1918-1984) is my hero. He quietly resisted the Jim Crow requirement of accepting a subservient consciousness. Alonzo was the second of five children born to Lelia and George Russell, May 18, 1918, in Smyth County, Virginia. He was a tall, unassuming, and gentle man. He belonged to the American Legion and the Oddfellows but was not much of a church goer.

Daddy was always a very giving man. He helped those in need. His most interesting service to others was to drive the family of the bereaved each time there was a funeral among the colored. I can never remember a time that he did not take off from work to perform this service. I thought it odd, but perhaps he was only abiding by the traditional African custom of paying tribute to the deceased.

To me, this light brown skin man with wavy hair, on which he used a stocking cap to keep in place, was the most handsome man I had ever seen. I called him "my pretty daddy". Frank McCollough, a close friend of his, would tease me unmercifully and bring me to tears when he referred to Daddy as "your old ugly daddy." I would retort, with tear-filled eyes, "My daddy is pretty."

While Daddy could read and write, he never finished high school. I surmise that he had to leave school to help out on the family farm, as he became of age during the Depression. I can only imagine what life was like for blacks during those years in the small Virginia town. His early years were spent farming and helping his father to trade and train show horses. I often wondered what tribe his father came from in Africa; the men all tall and handsome were excellent horsemen.

Even my two aunts, Helen and Gladys were expert riders.

My father and his younger brother, Thomas, were drafted to serve in WWII, while the eldest, James kept the farm running. Daddy was assigned to an all-black regiment, as was the case for all blacks during the War. He was stationed at Ft. Myers and Venice, Florida. It was during this time that he met my mother in Punta Gorda, where all the black soldiers would come on the weekends.

Daddy never talked much about the war, only to say that his lung became infected as a result of sleeping on the damp ground in camp, and that he met his brother Thomas on the ship on the return to the United States. Daddy was very lucky. He did not see combat; on the day that he was shipped out, the end of WWII was declared.

Daddy didn't talk about race. The only time that I ever heard of his reaction to the issue was when he quit a job because of unequal pay. Daddy got along well and had genuine relationships with both coloreds and whites. He, for many years, drove and delivered bricks for the brick factory in Marion. For coloreds this was a good job, that provided a decent blue-collar salary for him. He and another driver, Ferguson who was white, became good friends and often shared beer and conversation. One weekend evening while talking over beer, Ferguson revealed how much he made; he and Daddy had the same identical job title and Ferguson made twice as much as Daddy. He was livid, not at Ferguson, but at the idea of his being paid less. He walked in the office on Monday, asked for equal pay, was denied, and calmly walked to his car and came home. As I can recall, despite the uncertainty of the situation, mother supported my father in his decision, and I only a youngster thought of him as some sort of hero, for being so brave.

My father, being a good worker found a new job almost immediately. Daddy worked as a bartender and chauffeur for years. In the 1960s, a new opportunity came for him. He was hired as Driver at the Blue Ridge Job Corps for Girls in Marion. Daddy known at the Job Corps as "Lon" received employee recognition awards over the years, but it was his passion for baseball and a new talent coaching the girls' softball team and often being in the role of surrogate father that led to his greatest achievement as a colored man. Even today, girls whom he counseled praise him for his assistance during their years of growth. One year after Daddy's death, the activity building at the Blue Ridge Job Corps was named the "Russell Hall" in honor of my father.

Because Daddy had resisted following the prescribed colored subservient role for him, but instead by simply leaving in his quiet manner, he displayed his authentic identity as a man who honored his self-worth. From my father I learned the power of knowing and respecting my self-worth as a colored.

There are so many things that I wish I knew about my father's inner feelings, being a colored man. I wished that I had asked him questions about growing up colored in a southern town, being in a segregated army, working for less pay, his act of courage. I would have wanted to know what change he saw in his lifetime and how he felt about it.

This essay is dedicated to my father, who was born May 18, 1918, and married my mother on the date of his birthday as well.

Coming Home

Birthday Party
Punta Gorda Old Colored Playground

First Holy Communion

First Holy Communion
Sacred heart Catholic Church
Punta Gorda, Florida

Andrews Compound
Punta Gorda

Punta Gorda

When I was ten years of age, we made a trip from Virginia to Florida that would contribute greatly to my empowerment as a colored girl. We returned to the home of my mother. Because of the congenital heart defect which my mother suffered, her doctor had sent her home to die. This was a most interesting trip. In Marion, there was no colored funeral home, Barnett's Funeral Home served the colored population. Two white drivers were responsible for finding bathrooms which we could use, getting us food (from the front door) and taking care of the needs of my mother (on the stretcher), my grandmother, and myself. This was probably the safest trip that I had ever taken as a colored girl.

Coming to Punta Gorda meant living in a predominately colored community, unlike the mixed neighborhood in which we had lived in Marion. One thing was clear, even though colored paid their taxes, Jim Crow rules determined that they should not have the luxury of paved streets, sidewalks, and streetlights like predominately white neighborhoods. It was only the lack of services that marked it as colored, homes indicated a mixture of financial resources; elaborate two story houses like that in which my grandfather was reared, moderate cottages, to shot-gun houses.

"Community" in my colored culture was not just a physical location, but a consciousness of "we" vs "I"; of "collectivism". There was a sense of interdependence. Sharing and cooperating were essential aspects of "community". As a child, I knew of no hunger or homelessness in my community. Fishing was plentiful and residents planted gardens and shared products. There were always plenty of citrus fruits and guavas to share as well.

There was a sense of vitality as we passed through the colored business district, a sense of comfort in a separate all colored village. The smiles, waves and hellos, "welcome home" felt like being wrapped loving arms. As a child, I could feel the love of the entire community or village. In our traditional African American culture, children were raised by the community. We children were the hope and the future of the community. All adults in the community were responsible for the development of our character. Any adult had the authority and the duty to reprimand a child for inappropriate behavior. There was absolutely no talking back to or sassing any adult in the community no matter what their status. The "parenting" relationship in the community helped us to gain an understanding of what was acceptable in the community. In my Punta Gorda community, I grew up in a loving, caring, and nurturing village that expected me to use my gifts and talents to "give back" to the community and to uplift my colored brothers and sisters.

In our segregated all-colored community, we experienced and expressed tremendous joy; from Sunday afternoon baseball games to fish fry's, church plays and gospel singing. Most popular was our "Down the Street", in our business district where patrons would dress to the "nines" to be seen, listen to music and dance to our local band as well as traveling bands, and colored folks came from surrounding areas to have a good time unmolested by the police.

Traveling While Colored

Jaha and Saba
Big Boy Restaurant, U.S. I-95 North

Traveling as a colored child has been my greatest adventure while also experiencing unlimited inconveniences. The colored travel experience during Jim Crow could involve frustration, indignities, and even danger. Each summer as my grandmother Martha traveled "up North" taking myself and my cousin Skippy, she prepared for the experience.

"Granny," as we affectionately called her, would hire one of her tenants (she rented rooms to fishermen and men working on roads in the area) to drive up to Delaware, Washington, D.C., or New York to visit family. The tires, engine, and water tank were checked thoroughly before the trip as she did not want to have a mishap or repair to be needed while on the unfriendly road. The driver was coached on maintaining the speed limit, especially in small rural towns, and being aware of law enforcement. Granny always packed a delicious lunch of fried chicken, fruits, pound cake and other goodies that would last us the entire trip North.

Our first stop was Jacksonville with a cousin. Granny always left a $20 bill under the scarf on the dresser. I often wondered if that was a ritual that all colored travelers followed. We got up early and traveled only in the daylight. We had to make our next stop with family by dark. My grandmother was not aware of the "Green Book" that guided the travel of colored during Jim Crow.

Our gas tank was never less than half-filled as the driver would inquire if there was a colored restroom before filling up with gas. If there was a restroom, it was usually filthy. What excited my cousin and I most was stopping to take photos at state "Welcome" signs.

When we crossed the Mason-Dixon line, we were able to eat in restaurants on the freeway. Big Boy's was always our first stop, a tradition I followed with my own children.

My mother and I traveled from Florida to Virginia by train, of course going to the colored ticket window, and using the colored restroom in the small waiting area. We would be the last allowed to board the train, sitting in the colored car. When possible, we would have a meal in the small area of the dining car reserved for colored. As I recall, the excitement of travel, which remains with me some seventy years later, was a more powerful feeling than the indignities of segregation and discrimination.

My greatest anxiety, however, was reserved for my father who would travel by car to and from Virginia. While my family did not talk about being colored in America, the specter of violence always loomed, especially as it related to Daddy, a colored male. This was always a fearful time for my mother, myself, my whole family. Without fail, Daddy would be stopped in Jesup, Georgia. "Boy, you are driving too fast," or "Boy, you were driving too slow." Daddy learned to expect this and would carry enough extra money to pay the fine. This, however, was safer than his traveling alone on a rural road.

I can only imagine the fear that he must have felt, the imaginings that went through his head. My colored Daddy endured this each trip. He had to stand with head bowed, eyes lowered, voice passive. He swallowed the anger as he had been trained to do but at what cost? What did this do to his pride? As a man, how must he have felt having to play being subservient to another man, a man who in those moments had my father's life in his hands? But my father had no choice -- one wrong move could have cost him his life.

My greatest personal anxiety came when I had to ride the bus on Friday's for fifty miles from school in Sarasota to home in Punta Gorda for six years. That is another experience and another story.

The Reality of Being "Colored"

Image of Emmitt Till, Public Domain

When I was ten years of age, my world as a colored child was shaken. In Mississippi, fourteen-year-old Emmett Till was kidnapped, tortured, and brutalized to the extent that when his corpse was recovered, he was not recognizable. Like for most colored, and especially as a child, his disfigured face traumatized me. This was reality, however, of being colored in America, especially in Mississippi, that was considered an uncivilized state for coloreds.

I did not realize the degree to which I had been traumatized by Till's murder until some thirty years later. My husband, who was Ethiopian, and our five-year-old son and I were traveling from Florida to New Orleans. Passing through Mississippi, my son saw a sign indicating a road leading to a beach. Both my son and husband were eager to drive down to the beach. I had an immediate anxiety attack, the thought of driving down a country road in Mississippi was unbearable. My son was crying to go to the beach and my Ethiopian husband kept asking what was wrong with me as he continued down the road. When I saw another black family there, I was immediately relieved and returned to myself. I was not able to explain my strange reactions, neither my son nor my husband could have understood the fear I had experienced as a colored child in America, especially in the state of Mississippi.

I experienced fears from my days as a colored girl some forty years later when my son was older. While he had been away at college, we moved to a predominately white neighborhood. Jaha had gone to have breakfast with high school friends. I was scheduled to present a workshop in St. Petersburg. As usual, I turned on the alarm system. It wasn't until I was half-way across the Gandy Bridge (a bridge between Tampa and St. Petersburg) that I remembered that Jaha did not know the alarm code, I went into a panic. As soon as I got across the bridge I called the school, told them I had to go home because of a family emergency and would be late. Thoughts raced through my head of Jaha coming home, opening the door, the alarm going off, the police coming and not believing this was his home and the worst happening. I thanked God as I realized he had not come home yet. I stayed until he arrived and gave him the code. Being black, African American, or whatever we were designated did not matter, we were still the other and I feared for the life of my son.

A few months after he finished college, Jaha moved to Japan. I visited him there almost a year later and never worried again about his safety or well-being for the twenty years that he lived there and in Micronesia. He rarely came back to the US to visit; I went out there each year, when he did come home, I was happy to see him but not totally comfortable with his living back in the US.

While I do not consider myself to be "tragically colored," the fears of my ten-year old colored girl self were and are still deep in my psyche. The anniversary of the murders of Emmitt Till, Trayvon Martin, Michael Brown and Tamir Rice, revive the memories of days past. If racial violence continues to take the lives of young black males in this country, the reality of being "colored" remains despite the Civil Rights Act of 1964, and other "legal" measures that supposedly were indicators of America's racial progress.

The Value of Education

Baker Academy

Baker Academy

Just as my father and the women in my family had provided valuable lessons for my empowerment as a colored girl, so had my Punta Gorda community in laying a firm foundation to ensure my success and fulfill my potential. In the collective consciousness of my community, education was the key to the future of colored children. In all ways, the value of education was believed, stated, and demonstrated.

Education had been a core value since the community was founded. The first school was a Seventh-Day Adventist school operated by Mrs. Giles. Parents paid fifteen cents per week for their child to attend. Stories are told by elders that when a hurricane flooded the streets that men carried children on their backs to avoid them missing school. In 1902, Dan Smith, a colored community leader was sent to a convention to locate and hire a colored teacher. Residents pooled their finances to buy land on which to build the school. Baker Academy met the literacy needs of both children and adults in the early days. To ensure county funding for the school, adult men sat in classes with students to learn to read. By 1900, 70% of the residents could read, and 65% could read and write.

I attended Baker Academy, a four-room white frame schoolhouse named for its first teacher and principal, Benjamin Baker. The school, like the church, was a centerpiece of our community, it belonged to "us". There was community-wide support of Baker. Parents actively participated in school events, provided resources, time, and talents. There was collective support for our under-funded colored school.

When I attended Baker Academy, there were three teachers, Mrs. Smith who was the principal and taught grades 1 and 2; Mrs. Bailey 3 and 4; and Mrs. Clemons 5 and 6. The tiny "library" served as a lunchroom as well, restrooms were outside. These teachers provided the love, nurturing, encouragement, and discipline necessary for our future success as colored children. While each of these teachers had earned a Master's degree in Education, they were paid only half of what their white counterparts earned. After sixth grade, colored students were bussed past the white high school for the fifty-mile roundtrip to Dunbar High School in Fort Myers, Florida.

I never attended the new Baker and graduated from Booker High School in Sarasota in 1962. The Brown decision had no impact on my twelve years of attending colored schools. I was never the recipient as a colored student of equality in terms of the structure, supplies, resources, or even books that white students received.

The support of my Punta Gorda community provided this colored girl the motivation to prepare for the better future that education could provide for me. This hope made my weekly trips home on the Trailways bus bearable, as I anxiously prayed while waiting to board the bus after all the whites, that I would not have to stand for the 50 miles home or be subjected to sitting on the backseat with no personal space. This bus ride was a challenge that I faced and overcame because of the hopes and visions held for my future by my family and community.

The Back of the Bus

Trailways Bus

As I review my life as a colored girl, riding the Trailways bus on a weekly basis was my most uncomfortable and anxiety-producing experience. So, why was I riding the bus on a weekly basis?

Our colored Baker Academy only went to sixth grade. The colored students were bussed past the white high school to Dunbar High School in Fort Myers, a fifty-mile round trip. Besides having to get up and catch a bus by seven in the morning, Punta Gorda students were denied the full school experience related to extracurricular activities. The boys who played sports had to find and pay for their own transportation back to Punta Gorda.

My mother, Bernice, wanted me to have the full school experience, academics and extra-curricular activities denied to bus riders. She made a simple request to the school board at the end of the 1956 school year. She asked that I receive monies for room and board to live with my Aunt Ruth, a teacher at Booker High School in Sarasota. Mother was, of course, denied that request; they said that if they did that for me, they would have to do it for every colored student who requested it. To satisfy my mother, who was an active member of the NAACP, and to quell any intention that my mother might bring up the 1954 Brown decision, they quickly placed two portables at Baker for the 7th and 8th graders. A few years later, they built a new Baker Academy as many southern school districts were doing for fear that the colored would push for school desegregation. The new Baker was indeed substantially better than the old Baker Academy. Now colored students had a library, a cafeteria, and even were able to have a band.

I never attended Baker in the portables or the new school. For six years, 7-12 grade, I attended Booker High School in Sarasota. Each Friday, I took the 6:30 bus to Punta Gorda, except when I wished to stay over for a football game or was able to get a ride home. I was saved from having to ride the bus back on Sunday by the pastor of my grandmother's church who lived in Sarasota.

"Back of the bus, back seat" and headache or nausea from the exhaust describe my experience for those six years. Each week, I stood at the back of the line with other colored to wait to board the bus, then with anxiety in my heart and mind, hoped that the last two rows of seats before the back seat would not be taken by whites. I was lucky sometimes and at other times not. I don't remember ever having to stand up for the fifty-mile trip but the lack of any sense of personal space was most depressing and uncomfortable. The continuous smell of exhaust made me nauseous.

Some sixty or so years later, I am still uncomfortable taking a bus.

The backseat of the bus to this colored girl was intended as a disregard for our humanity, the view that we were one undeserving entity, not separate individuals, whose discomfort felt when encroachment in our personal space occurred was immaterial because we were not truly human.

Empowering Lessons for a Colored Girl

Martha

The most empowering lessons I have learned about myself, my life, and my future were learned during the Jim Crow era when I was labeled a "colored". These lessons were of four types: those of denial, affirmation, protection, and character building. The family, community (village) and school each provided and reinforced the values we as children should learn as well as the expectations held for us.

The "denials" were critical in helping us as "colored" children to know our true identity:
- "I am not tragically colored."
- "I am not who the larger white society believes or says that I am."
- "I am not inferior to any race or group, culturally, intellectually, or morally."
- "I am not the "other" whom they claim that I am, undeserving of respect, dignity, and equality."

The "affirmations" confirmed our true identity:
- "I know who I am."
- "I am a precious gift to my family and community."
- "I am a member of a dynamic culture that provides for my well-being and joy."
- "I am born with unique gifts and talents that I will use to better my community and fulfill my life purpose."

As a colored child, it was also crucially important that I learned protective lessons during the Jim Crow era. There were the Jim Crow laws related to segregation that we were to obey, but in addition, there were the Jim Crow customs or etiquette that served to enhance the identity and esteem of whites. Colored people had two forms of identity during this period, a "performance identity" in the form of subservient attitude, speech, and demeanor that reinforced a sense of superiority among whites. As a colored child, I learned that whites expected certain behaviors that I must oblige to protect myself from their wrath. I saw what I call a "performance identity" demonstrated by colored adults. They might stand with head bowed, making no eye contact, and speaking in a subservient tone to a white person. However, in demonstrating what I call their "authentic identity" that same person might be the most esteemed and well-spoken deacon in their church, or the mother of the church who organized and coordinated church events. These individuals might also be those in our community who taught and demonstrated the values that we as colored children must learn. We respected these adults in both roles because we as children understood how crucial our making whites feel that we believed in our own inferiority was during this era. We learned that we were never to appear smarter than or dispute the word of whites. We knew to be back in our community by dusk and to avoid groups of whites.

"I am because we are." - African proverb

Our character building began in the family in the form of what we called "home training". "Home training was the cultural vehicle by which values were

transmitted to each new generation. The very same values that had been instilled in my mother were now being learned by this little colored girl. We were taught what is right or wrong, good or bad behavior. We as children learned the social rules and norms that would guide our conduct as members of the community from childhood to adulthood. A child's behavior was a demonstration of the quality of home training a colored child received. These lessons had to build our character, to learn respect and proper manners. The core rules of home training were:
- Respect yourself.
- Respect your family.
- Respect the elderly.

A family's name was very important, and we were taught and expected not to do anything to bring shame upon ourselves or our family. Respect for elders was most important. In our African tradition, ancestors were very highly respected, and our elders were considered to be closest to the ancestors. Good manners were expected of us as children. There were women in our community who took responsibility for teaching etiquette and manners to us.

Unlike the stereotype of the colored as being unsocialized and incapable of living in a civilized society, our character as colored children was developed to the highest extent. We were taught what is right or wrong, good or bad behavior. We as children learned the social rules and norms that would guide our conduct as members of the community from childhood to adulthood. A child's behavior was a demonstration of the quality of home training a colored child received. Home training made us a "collective being"; we learned behaviors that would help us live harmoniously and cooperatively with others. Who I am today, my moral character, my ability to interact and form relationships with people of cultures other than my own is the result of the "home training" or socialization I received as a colored girl.

The Road Ahead...

1962
Class Valedictorian
Booker High School - Sarasota, Florida

In 1962, I graduated from Booker High School in Sarasota, Florida, proudly as my class Valedictorian. Those years had not been without sacrifice by me, like my mother, I lived with a relative to complete high school, rather than taking the 50-mile roundtrip to attend Dunbar High School in Fort Myers.

While the perception of a colored school, teachers, and students was one of inferiority; I received a superior education that provided me the competency, confidence, and commitment to excellence to go out into the wider society.

The next step, going to college was not an option for me, it was a certainty. The role designed for a colored girl who only completed high school was to do domestic work of some sort. In the early 1960s, I could not become a teller in the bank, a clerk in a store, or an entry-level employee in a government or corporate office.

The reality of what was expected of me as a colored girl was made perfectly clear when I was only thirteen years old. My mother always very proud of her daughter was telling a group of white women that I had completed my typing course. One of the women, surprisingly asked my mother if I could come and do some typing for her, my mother agreed as I typed for residents in my neighborhood. When I arrived at the woman's house, she guided me to a bucket to wash windows rather than a typewriter. To say the least, I was shocked, but assumed the colored "performance identity," moving very slowly with the task. I used some excuse to give my mother a call. Hearing what was occurring, mother came immediately to pick me up.

I left without saying a word to the woman. My mother was angry that the woman had lied. I on the other hand felt pity for the woman, a white woman so insecure of her "place" in society that she would be threatened by a 13-year-old child learning a skill rather than being condemned to a menial work life. The lessons learned from my grandmother Martha (Granny) self-determination, and my mother Bernice, self-worth, provided me with consciousness and power that the woman's gesture to "put me in my place" had no effect, rather it fueled my determination to go to college and show all who I was destined to become.

I lived with my aunt Ruth, who held a Master's Degree in Biology and was known by all as a superior teacher. She modeled all that I, as a colored woman who possessed a college degree, should be. Ruth was committed to excellence in every way; she never stopped learning and applying her new skills to "give back" to her Sarasota community. Mrs. Spires" was a well-known and respected colored teacher who always went above and beyond in expecting only excellence from her students.

The three C's: competency, confidence, and commitment to excellence was expected of the students who attended my segregated colored school, despite the inequalities we experienced. With only one microscope in our lab, I was equipped to master biological science in college, with few and used books, the "pushing" of my English teacher, made it possible for me to win first place in two county-wide essay contests. I left Booker High School to attend a predominately white university in the Midwest, a university five times the size of the "little fishing village" from which I came, and never missed a beat. No, there was no Affirmative Action at the time, I was simply a product of committed and masterful teachers, most holding graduate degrees.

As I was now going out into the wider world, leaving the security of my encouraging and nurturing community, all my experiences, even the inconvenient and sometimes traumatizing ones prepared me for my life ahead. I was to show the world who I was, the truth of my identity, not "tragically colored, but an empowered colored girl ready for the challenges I would face.

"Granny"

Martha Long Andrews

Martha and Martha (Granny)

My grandmother, Martha Andrews, was central in influencing my true identity. She had a saying of "that doesn't mean us." We of course had to obey Jim Crow laws or we would be punished. However, we were never to give up our human dignity by going to the back of a restaurant or shopping where we were not respected.

My grandmother, for whom I am named, when asked about her race or ethnic background, would say that "I'm a third, a third, a third." She was the daughter of a full-blooded Cherokee Indian, and a father whose mother was an enslaved woman of color and her white master. She respected all aspects of her bloodline. My grandmother was a woman who was very respected by colored and whites, she had both as close friends.

"Granny," as I called her, taught me that I could achieve anything in life that I wanted. She did. Granny had three life goals: to have a family, to become a nurse (her mother was a midwife), and to visit the Holy Land. She had her family and lived a very prosperous life. She left Jackson County, Florida at an early age, she did not graduate from high school. It is doubtful that there was a high school for her to attend. She like others of her age group attended night school classes for adults held at Baker Academy in Punta Gorda. She earned a correspondence school certificate that allowed her to do private duty nursing. In her elder years, she and her cousins went to the Holy Land.

My grandmother was a very giving woman who followed the cultural traditions of taking care of elders in the community. She built a house and cared for an elder without family in the community. Granny believed in her humanity and that of other colored people. She was one of three people who formed the first NAACP in our community.

Believing as she did in her autonomy and experiencing her personal power, after her death, I discovered in her desk Mayan magazines and even information related to the Rosicrucians. Martha was a colored woman who through her beliefs about herself, defined her own identity, achieved her goals, and explored horizons that one would never expect. My "granny" as a role model for me of a colored woman influenced my life choices in many ways.

Mommy

Bernice Andrews Russell

Bernice – Ladies' Auxiliary
American Legion

Bernice on Mural in Punta Gorda

Bernice Russell

Bernice – Receiving Rotary "Service Above Self" Award 1997

Bercnie – Ladies' Auxiliary

Bernice – Guild of Our Lady

In my formative years as a colored girl, I was taught through stories, lectures, and role modeling two of our most important values. Preserving and promoting "community" is a paramount value that I was taught in my Punta Gorda community. Every individual had a stake and responsibility in using their gifts and talents to give back to the community. The values of community and giving back were essential to colored people creating successful institutions and vibrant business communities.

Our community was like one large family. Each person, even children, understood that they had a part in making the community work. Families shared vegetables grown in gardens as well as oranges, grapefruits, mangoes, and guavas from their trees. Fishermen shared their catches. Men helped each other build houses, women made quilts together, those with cars transported those without, and children were expected to obey all adults and honor their elders, in particular.

My mother Bernice Andrews Russell, whose image is painted on a mural in the center of Punta Gorda, was my example of the colored woman that a colored girl like me must aspire to be. Born in Marianna, Florida, the home of her mother Martha, Bernice was raised in Punta Gorda. Bernice was very proud of her heritage because she was the granddaughter of pioneer James Andrews, the first fireman (fire engineer) at the Ice House, and the niece of city pioneer Daniel Smith, whose wife Louisa, was the sister of her grandmother, Queen Andrews.

Bernice loved and aspired to be like her grandmother Queen. Queen lived in one of the three two-story houses in the neighborhood. Queen was a very elegant woman. She had a piano in her home, and used her china to entertain. Queen was the example of a "colored" woman that Bernice wanted to emulate. Queen in no way fit the stereotype of the uncultured, sex-crazed colored woman bandied about by whites.

Bernice attended Baker Academy in Punta Gorda. There was no colored high school, therefore Bernice had to live with her mother's uncle in Ocala, Florida to attend high school. She earned her diploma from Howard Academy. After graduation, Bernice went to Florida Agricultural & Mechanical College (Florida A&M) where she took an electrical course. Bernice did not receive a college degree, which she regretted, but her options were limited. She did not want to be a teacher, and due to congenital heart problems, she could not pass the physical requirement to enter the nursing program, which was her greatest desire. She was, however, able to repair anything from lamps to irons to other appliances. Had she not been colored and a female, she might have become an electrician.

When WWII came along, so did Alonzo Russell, my father who literally swept her off her feet. Bernice and Alonzo's attempt to get a marriage license is an example of the type of mutually respectful relationships that existed between colored and white pioneer families in Punta Gorda. Judge Rose called my grandfather to ask if he knew his daughter was getting married. Judge Rose felt he should be sure my grandfather knew their plans, though my mother was twenty years of age.

In 1955, because of her heart condition, she was told she had one year to live. As a result of this diagnosis, she returned to Punta Gorda with me. She worked as a "housekeeper" for Harry Carpenter for many years, she never referred to or thought of herself as a "maid." It wasn't until after the 1964 Civil Rights Act was passed that Bernice was hired by the County to work in Senior Services. Bernice established the first congregate meal program for seniors in Charlotte County in Punta Gorda.

With the beliefs and values fostered in the community, Bernice began her role as community advocate. My mother expressed and demonstrated who I should become as an educated colored woman. I remember her selling hot dogs and sodas, during weekend dances for the colored youth to have entertainment and to raise money to buy chairs for our new Cooper Street Recreation Center, as the City provided only the empty building for the colored community. Bernice volunteered as a bingo caller for the American Legion of which she belonged, and in time became President of the Women's Auxiliary.

In the magazine, Mature Lifestyles, Bernice was referred to as "Mother Theresa" of the colored community. "Why can't they just say Mother Theresa of Punta Gorda?" Bernice asked. This was so true because Bernice "gave back" to the entire Punta Gorda community. It was to Bernice, that folks came to for advice and assistance. Accessible and acceptable housing was of great importance to Bernice, as a result, she was appointed as Vice Chairperson of the Punta Gorda Housing Authority. Over the years, I watched her dedication to serving her community -- she received many awards. Her greatest honor was presented to her by the Rotary Club for "service above self."

My mother taught me to use my talents and abilities to serve my community. While she regretted not getting a college education, she knew how to tap into and use her leadership skills. She was either President or Vice President of every organization of which she was a member. She also made it very clear to me, that if a colored girl like myself got a good education, and became a "buppy" (an upwardly mobile young colored) that I would be wasting a good education. My mother's sister, my Aunt Ruth, who did earn a college degree, preached the same sermon, "How would I serve?" as she did in her Sarasota community.

This essay is dedicated to my mother Bernice and my Aunt Ruth, who were role models for the value of "giving back, lifting as we climbed."

Bernice and Sister Ruth Spires

Ruth, Martha, Bernice

"Negro" or "negro"

Anitta Rutherford Orr

"I believe that eight million Americans are entitled to a capital letter." W.E.B. Du Bois

Social equality is the demon that cannot be tolerated within the tenets of white supremacy. Even capitalizing the "N" in Negro was a violation of this premise in the world of white supremacy. A capital N would give a respect that could equate with some type of social recognition, while the small "n" was a symbol of the low "place" that the group held in the racial hierarchy of American white society.

In 1962, I was off to college "up North," as we called the Midwest. While the Jim Crow laws and customs prevalent in the South had not disempowered the spirit of this colored girl, it would be refreshing to leave behind the "Colored and White" designations and southern society itself. I was looking forward to being allowed to evolve into a "Negro."

A rude awakening occurred, however, during my travels to college, which made me aware of W.E.B. Du Bois's concern about the small (n) or capital (N) in my racial designation. My mother, aunt, and I had to sleep in the car in Terra Haute, Indiana, as no motel would accommodate us. I intimately understood that while I was officially a Negro in the North, in many circumstances, I would still be treated as a "negro."

My new home as a Negro was Western Michigan University in Kalamazoo, Michigan. I was assigned a Negro roommate as was the custom; we were told we would be more comfortable with our own. I had good friends and relationships my entire stay in the dorm, but my social life was usually confined to other Negroes.

Negrohood was evident in most aspects of life at Western. We organized our own dances and other social activities. In the Student Union, Negro students had their own special area, called "tac corner," where we gathered.

The Greek system was prominent at Western for both white and Negro students. I pledged Delta Sigma Theta sorority wherein most of my social life took place. It was through my Negro sorority that my earlier lessons at home in the South as a colored girl were reinforced. Delta Sigma Theta was a service sorority -- the value of "giving back," something I already knew, was central. As a pledge, I had a leadership role in planning a career fair for Negro students in Kalamazoo.

The small "n" was present in our relationships at Western subtly, most of the time, but often enough it was quite overt. On one occasion, our big sisters demanded that we eight pledges spend the night together. Because both my roommate and I were pledging, we decided that the other six should slip into our room for the evening. Of course, we were discovered and reprimanded, the house limit per person per room being two. The housemother implied that our prank was a demonstration of our moral inferiority: we were accused of stealing $6 from the dormitory, as the cost was $1 per guest. The real issue was not the $6, which the pledges could have paid, but that the dormitory policy said that only one guest was allowed overnight in a dorm room. As if sorority pranks were not carried on by white girls, ours was regarded as a demonstration of our "negroness."

The belief in our "negroness" in cultural and intellectual inferiority was not confined to dorm mothers but was demonstrated by a professor. At a time when Negroes were considered unable to speak Standard English, three Negro students were enrolled in the Speech and Hearing program at Western. The professor of Phonetics informed one of the Negro students that she would probably fail the Phonetics class because Negroes did not hear sounds in the same way as whites did. However, because she had learned the same lessons in the North as I had learned as a colored girl in the South, she understood that she simply had to show him who she truly was. This Negro student, Anitta Rutherford Orr, not only passed the class but became a supervisor in the Speech and Hearing program in the Detroit Public Schools. Even more telling of who she was, Anitta Rutherford Orr became President of the Michigan Speech and Hearing Association. She was obviously not "tragically colored."

As I evolved into my capital-N, Negro consciousness, I realized that the lessons I learned as a colored girl were coming to the fore as the most helpful and empowering characteristics to continue to cultivate as I grew up. My group and I would be perceived and treated as "negroes" rather than "Negroes," but we would continue to show our stuff: who we had been reared to be - strong, resilient, never depending on others to define us.

"Culturally Deprived"?

Baker Academy
Spring Performance

Etiquette Dinner for Community Youth

My most shocking revelation related to being a Negro in a white society came in an educational course. I could not believe the words that I was seeing; that I and my ethnic group were "culturally deprived." There it was: a scholarly article based upon mythology and ignorance of cultural differences.

Cultural deprivation is a sociological theory that asserts the notion that ethnic and social groups possess inferior values, norms, skills, and knowledge which places them at a disadvantage in the larger society. Cultural deprivation as it relates to Negro culture is a myth based on stereotypes of a group's cultural, intellectual, and moral existence.

It is the dynamic and empowering Negro culture that has made it possible for this Negro girl, despite segregation, discrimination, and lack of equal access to opportunities in the larger society, to succeed.

Resilience is described as the capacity to withstand and recover from adversity. Resilience provides the psychological strength to successfully adapt to and cope with struggle and hardship. Cultural resilience based upon collectivism rather than individualism has within it the innate capability of a cultural system of beliefs, values and, norms that will enable individuals and communities to overcome adversity.

Cultural resilience in the Negro culture is the result of spirituality, our complete faith and trust in the Creator; the traditional values of hope transmitted by ancestors; a collective community consciousness; and our racial identity.

- Spirituality: the church is a key institution in the community -- a strong belief in access to spiritual energy, the release of fear, and the expectation of good and joy. Religious services include clapping, which releases stress, provides healing energy, and a belief that moving stirs the spirit.
- Hope: the bridge of the past to the future; the sharing of community values and accomplishments by elders. Elders provide models, stories, and achievements despite obstacles. Storytelling is the oral tradition of overcoming. Hope is a belief in and expectancy in the future; it is the ability to see past the current situation and the expectation to preserve and promote the well-being of the community.
- Community consciousness of "we" versus "I" and the belief that "I am because we are" promote a sense of connection and interdependence, keys to resilience. The value of "giving back," providing a service to others in the community, provides an atmosphere of emotional release, the sense of freedom one derives from letting go of pain and fear by helping others.
- Ethnic Identity: knowing "who I am," my heritage and history; belief in the influence of our ancestors, their overcoming of and resistance to subjugation, and relying on

cultural traditions over generations, a cultural coping strategy.

Joy, the ability to laugh, sing, and dance despite racial oppression and violence is an expression of cultural resilience. As a people, we choose joy as an expression of freedom. Joy is our resistance against negative stereotypes and our conscious decision to celebrate who we are as a people. Our food, families, music, provide joy as they support and uplift us. In our separate societies within our overall population, we have the freedom to create and express our authentic selves, unfiltered, all of which promotes our joy and capacity to not only survive but to thrive despite the obstacles and oppressions we experience.

Current research suggests that African Americans may be more resilient than white Americans. Studies suggest that while white Americans on the average are the healthiest group in the society, as a group, they are far less resilient than African Americans. Resilience, the keystone of Negro culture, refutes myths characterizing the culture as deficient.

I graduated from Western Michigan University with my major in Speech and Hearing Therapy and was encouraged to pursue a Master's degree. This Negro girl had no idea that my racial designation and sense of self-definition would evolve widely very soon.

1966
Alonzo, Martha, Bernice
Graduation from Western Michigan University

The Essayist

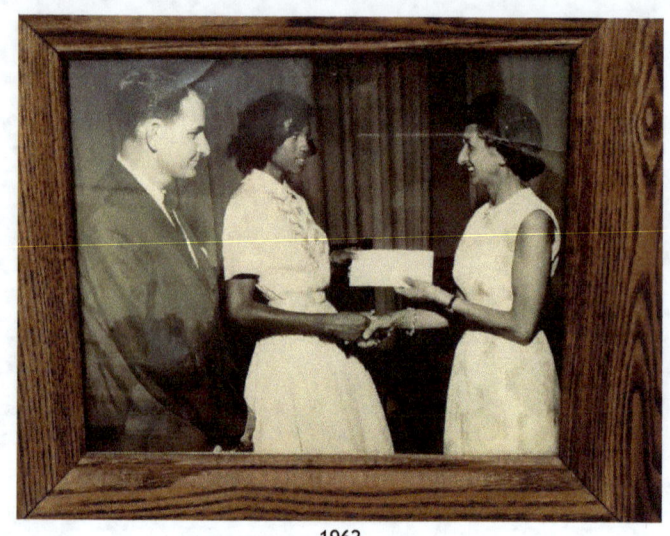

1962
Martha Receiving The Civitan Club Award
Best Essay: What Democracy Means to Me

She was sixteen, sheltered, and shy. But, she was smart, Valedictorian of her class. She loved writing and hoped to become a journalist. Her English teacher, Mrs. Daily, encouraged her writing and entered her into contests. She won both the Optimist Club and the Civitan Club essay competitions her senior year. Winning the Civitan award was special because she received a $50 savings bond.

That year's topic was "What Democracy Means to Me." In the untested heart and mind of the essayist, the amazing sixties vitalized her, a Negro girl growing up in the Jim Crow south: The Brown decision had outlawed school segregation, Negroes had won the right to sit where they chose since the Montgomery bus boycotts, Negro college students were engaged in freedom rides and sit-ins at lunch counters. Young Dr. Martin Luther King, Jr. had sparked the fire of freedom in generations of Negroes.

A required course for all senior students, "Democracy vs Communism," prepared her well to pen an essay about what Democracy meant to her. She had learned thoroughly the oppressive system of communism, its lack of freedom, justice, and the individual's aching for a better life that only democracy promised. She wrote eloquently about the free and fair elections promised by democracy, somehow ignoring the fact of Negroes were killed for registering to vote. She wrote sincerely of human rights and equal protection under the law, though she had been ten years of age and aware when Emmett Till was murdered in Mississippi. The essayist wrote of social equality, overcome with the prospect while also knowing deep down that she, her parents, ancestors, or any other Negro that she knew and knew of had not exactly experienced it.

She wrote it even as she was aware of the fear that her parents could not protect her from harm.

But here was the opportunity to share her dream of the goodness of America. She poured out her soul, her vision of her country as the great democracy where each and every citizen was free to live the dream. She wrote convincingly of things that neither she nor anyone she knew had full access to.

When it was time to go to college, the essayist's family insisted that she choose something more practical for a Negro girl than journalism. They suggested that with only the magazines "Jet" and "Ebony" as possible employers, she might find her education wasted. Surely, she did not want to join the ranks of the majority of Negro women as domestic servants. They wanted more for her. She chose Speech Pathology as a major, minoring in English. At her university, only one journalism course was taught. She took it as an elective, happy to write for the university newspaper. Who wouldn't be thrilled to publish a front-page article? It was an interview of Saul Alinsky, the radical community organizer and writer.

That was the last article she would write for fifty years. During the Civil Rights movement, she stayed safely in the North while others braver than she were beaten, spit upon, thrown in jail in the South. She swallowed the anger but never became so full as to express it on paper. However, during each presidential election cycle thereafter, she wondered what it would be like to experience interviewing and writing about the candidates. But, she did not have the courage of her convictions. She let go of her dream and decided her family was right, better to get the best life you could as a Negro, well, Black, by then. She also was not ready to suffer the indignities of being the "first" Black.

In 1967, after experiencing the Detroit Riot, she came home for a visit, full of the rage of almost all Blacks of her age. She pulled out the essay of which her mother was so proud and tore it into shreds in front of her parents' unbelieving eyes. Now a young adult, painfully aware of what it meant to be Black in America, she could not believe she had written such sappy, ignorant thoughts about a concept that had no meaning or relevance for her. She hated herself for allowing whites to believe that she dreamed or hoped for what was theirs alone. She hated most that in her eagerness to impress she had surely fostered their sense of superiority; poor little Negro girl hoping for something she could never have.

In 1990, she wrote her first book, one on co-dependency; and then two more related to the education of children of color. The writing was not the same as when she had been an essayist. What she wrote now was scholarly, devoid of the purity of soul, the exposure of the spirit with which she had written decades before. Her naiveté was long gone. It would be some thirty-five years before she wrote an essay in which she could lay bare her soul again.

On her 71st birthday, she woke with the questions faced by many of her age. How had she lived her life? What had she accomplished? What was she proud of? What remained undone? She boasted of her greatest accomplishment -- two Ivy League-educated children -- the Dartmouth son, a city councilman; the daughter, a Harvard-educated lawyer. She, the good mother, had earned her Ph.D. and a successful career. She had published books, she had revived and directed a historical museum.

She remembered the essay of more than fifty years before. So long ago, she had dipped her foot in the water of racism, but in a clinical rather than a literary sense. Rather than becoming a journalist, using the written word, to describe the world she saw impacted by the virus of racism, she earned terminal degrees and developed her expertise in counseling individuals and groups. She had consulted and trained (various organizations) on issues of race, diversity, and gender for over thirty years. In this role, she created spaces where people could develop their cognitive independence and become protagonists in their lives. Because of the lessons learned as a colored girl, racism was not personal, it was not her problem, but the issue of those unfortunate souls whose esteem and emotional well-being needed to have race be a central aspect of their being.

America's cultural mind had been flooded with the images of Blackness created, reinforced, and perpetuated. Now at 71, she was ready to free the essayist of her credulous youth, to express her mind, to let her spirit leap onto the pages. This time, it would be different: yes, she would write essays again, but not those of the hopeful dupe of a Negro girl she was in the early '60s. These essays would be the truth of an experienced elder who understood the realities of America's grand democracy.

She knew what she had to say.

Redefining My Identity

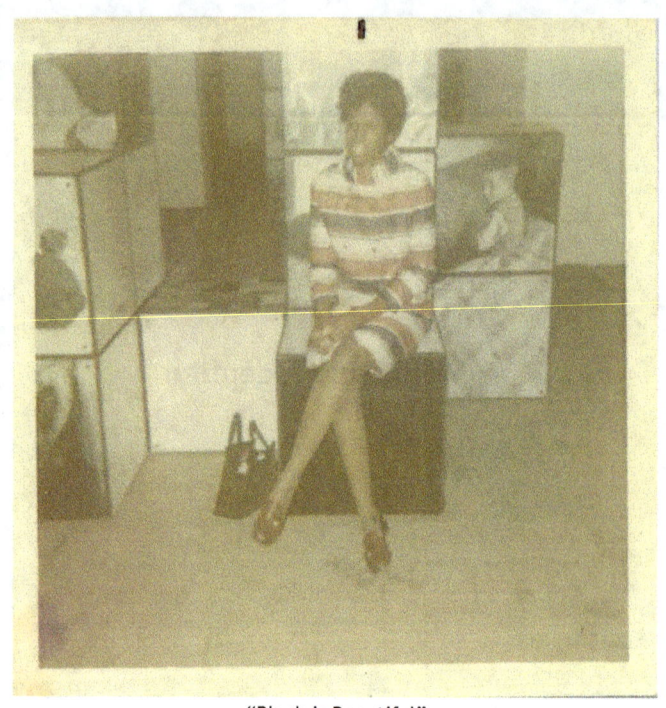
"Black is Beautiful"
Afro

Granny, Cousin Carrie, Martha

Teaching - Afro

Bernice - Afro

The year 1966 proved to be monumental in my racial definition. It was the year that I became "Black."

Only months after I received my undergraduate degree, Stokely Carmichael shouted "Black Power" and instantly changed not only my racial identity but my consciousness. In October of 1966, Huey P. Newton and Bobby Seale created the Black Panther Party, which would impact the consciousness of all Black Americans and America itself.

Even more than the Civil Rights Movement, the Black Power Movement has had the most significant impact on the consciousness of those of us designated as "Black," "inferior," "inhuman" and the "other." The Black Power Movement refuted the ideology of white superiority and Black inferiority; it made "Blackness" a consciousness of power rather than a label of victimhood. Those "Black" in consciousness did not have to assimilate, acculturate, or be accepted by white society. Black Power taught us that Blackness is its own beauty, agency, and power.

Before the Black Power Movement, many "coloreds" and "Negroes" were as disdainful of Black skin as whites. There were fights resulting from being called "Black" and nicknames such as "Smoky" or "Blue" given to those with very dark skin. Even today, there are Black adults who because of skin-color harassment as children hate themselves and other Black people. Even Negro institutions reinforced the belief that Black skin was inferior; top-ranked Negro colleges asked for photos on admission forms, and college queens were always "light, bright and almost white." Colorism was pervasive in the Negro community.

The consciousness of "Black Power" was not new. The agency of the obvious self-determination of Black communities during Jim Crow, erased from history books, were lost to us. What Stokely proclaimed had been present, though not so named, was alive and well in vibrant, self-sufficient and prosperous Black communities during the Jim Crow era. Without white direction or assistance, Black people had created dynamic educational, social, and business institutions that rivaled those in white society. Autonomous, segregated Black communities proved that Black inferiority was a myth. Stokely's call brought us out of our state of forgetfulness. We as a people became proud again – and maybe for the first time -- of who we were, what our culture meant to us and the power that we held.

The Black Power Movement of the 1960s and 1970s grew out of and along with the Civil Rights Movement, calling for a sense of self-determination and the independent development of social and political institutes for Black people. Black Power emphasized racial pride and self-reliance rather than integration. Black Power focused on building power in our own as a people rather than seeking accommodation from white power structures. It promoted solidarity and using our collective power to determine our future in this society.

The Black Power Movement promoted racial pride, self-respect and the acknowledgement of the beauty and dynamism of our culture. The Black Power Movement promoted the creation of Black political and cultural institutes, the demand for Black history courses, and Black bookstores. We as a people became self-focused as a race in all respects -- our art, literary pursuits, and music as much as our financial and political growth. James Brown sang, "I'm Black and I'm Proud." Most pronounced to me as a former colored girl, was our definition of beauty: "Black is beautiful," and our afros were the rage.

Most critically to me, the call for Black Power reverberated in my consciousness, for it was already this colored girl's self-identity, self-worth, and self-determination. These character traits had been slowly, deliberately, and consciously given to me all my life as the norm – for me – in the era of segregation and prejudice. It was however, with the Black Power Movement that I embraced it openly and proudly.

The call for Black Power renewed my sense of self as I crystalized the lessons of self-identity, self-worth and self-determination learned from family and community. First, my own family and then, my segregated education by dedicated colored teachers came to the fore in my consciousness and allowed my already honed sense of competency and confidence to burst out into the expectation that I pursue excellence in my every endeavor.

What Does It Mean to be American?

Jaha and Saba

Jaha and Saba

A Trip to Tarpon Springs

In 1988, Rev. Jesse Jackson began a movement to change the designation of "Black" to "African American", to symbolize Black Americans' historical connection to the continent. The designation of "African American" was the first-time Blacks in the United States had been acknowledged as Americans.

There was disagreement however, among some Blacks who believed that they had no connection to Africa, rather 300 years of American heritage. While Blacks may not know their definite ethnic group from which they descend, Africa was the place of their ancestors. Blackness is a social/political designation, the opposite of whiteness created over 300 years ago to establish the place of Blacks in the social/racial hierarchy of American society. This raises a question.

What does it mean to be American? Being an American is the belief that everyone has access and opportunity to achieve success in the United States through hard work, no matter their background. America prides itself on being a "meritocracy," a society in which persons achieve success based on demonstrated merit. Merit is demonstrated as a result of individual ability and talent.

The educational system is crucial in providing equal opportunity so that the abilities and talents of all students can be recognized and nurtured to demonstrate the merit essential for success in achieving the American dream. Is it possible however, that conditioned stereotypical beliefs based upon the myth of African American intellectual inferiority can prevent teachers from recognizing and acknowledging innate abilities that would later demonstrate merit?

Unfortunately, as two middle-class African American parents, both holding graduate degrees, we saw the abilities or merit of our children denied. My son Jaha was recommended to be tested for the gifted program when he became of age as both a kindergartner and first-grader. We approached the school and were not given a response; after continued inquiry, we were told that his records had been lost. Finally understanding that we would have my son tested by psychologists at the university where my husband worked, the school relented. My son was finally tested, and the school psychologist reported that he scored higher than anyone else tested. Our problems were not over however, Jaha was having difficulty in his gifted math class. His instructor suggested that perhaps he had been misplaced and did not belong in a gifted math class. Being a speech and hearing specialist, I knew that checking the eyes and ears of a student having difficulty was the first option. My son needed glasses and it did not help that the teacher had him seated at the back of the classroom. With glasses, he excelled. We never told him of his teacher's misperceptions, rather encouraged him not to be beaten by math.

My daughter Saba, after continued inquiry, was tested for the gifted program, and enrolled as well. She was recruited by top universities and admitted to Stanford. In front of her English class, the teacher whose daughter had applied but not been accepted, suggested that my daughter got into Stanford based upon some criteria other than her merit. My daughter had every merit that Stanford was seeking, an honor student, excellent writer, and leader in many extra-curricular activities.

If the legitimacy of the merits of two African American children from a home, with the opportunities our children had to develop abilities and talents, were not recognized, what about the masses of African American children?

It was my experience as an African American parent seeing how the conditioned narrative of African American intellectual inferiority functioned in the educational system that propelled me to begin work as a consultant dealing with issues related to the perception and treatment of African American students in our schools. Again, I must ask, "What does it mean to be an American?" Does the American designation following African have true meaning?

Education: A Tool to Empower or A Weapon to Disempower

Consulting and Training with School Districts

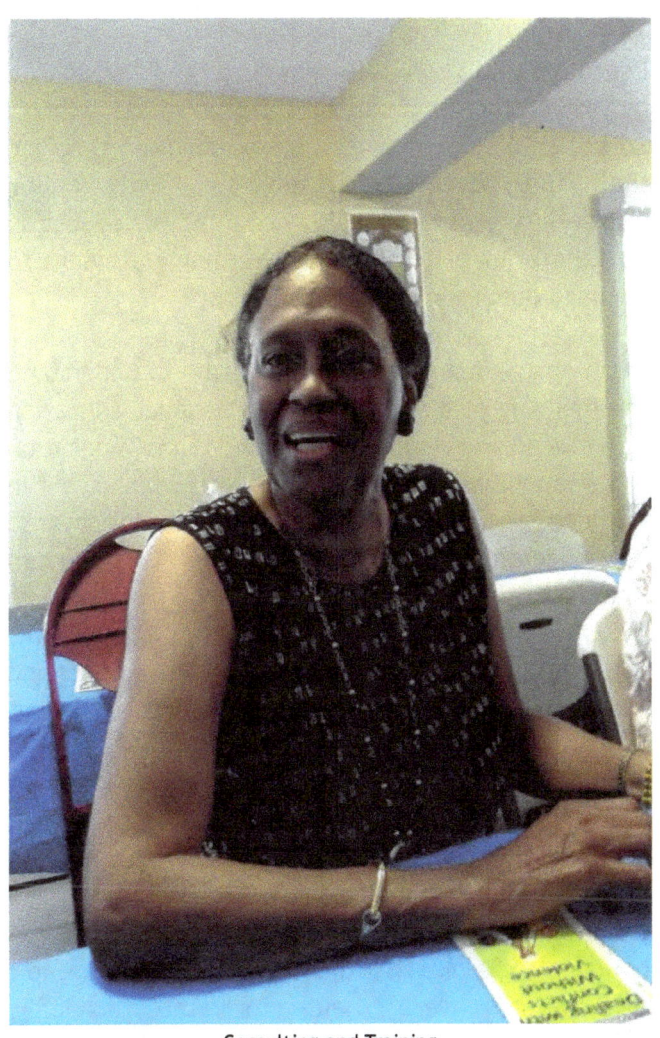

Consulting and Training

"Education is the most powerful weapon which you can use to change the world." - Nelson Mandela

Education was a core value cherished and transmitted by my colored family, community, and school. Education was the key to colored children reaching their full potential, a tool for racial uplift, citizenship, and leadership. Acquiring an education was the primary tool of empowerment, a means to gaining equality in American society.

As an African American parent, I came to understand the meaning of an additional quote about education as a weapon attributed to Joseph Stalin: "Education is a weapon, whose effect depends on who holds it in his hands and to whom it is aimed." This insight into how education could be used to disempower African American children influenced my career path. In 1992, I founded an education consulting company, with the purpose of transforming the perspectives and academic expectations held by educators about African American students.

The stereotypical belief in the cultural, intellectual, and moral inferiority of African Americans was pervasive in the schools in which I consulted and trained. The culture of African American parents was believed to be one that did not value education; low expectations were held for the academic achievement of African American students, and African American males, in particular, were victims of racial disparity in disciplinary actions.

On May 17, 1954, the Supreme Court declared in its landmark decision, Brown v. Board of Education, that segregated schooling based upon race was unequal and unconstitutional. The decision failed however, in not mandating that stereotypical beliefs about African Americans be refuted, and all educators required to demonstrate freedom from these beliefs. Unfortunately for many, this was not the case. African American students were placed and bussed in school environments in which they were denied access to equal educational opportunities. They were tracked into lower-level classes, overwhelmingly placed in special education classes, and denied access to gifted classes, as was the experience of my own son initially.

By the 1990s, schools across the United States had undergone a process of resegregation. This new form of segregation, emerging in the post-Brown era, had parallels to the past but also introduced unique challenges that detrimentally affected the academic drive and success of African American students. Like my colored segregated school, contemporary schools with majority "minority" and poor students, often contend with insufficient funding and limited educational resources. A stark contrast, however, is seen in the faculty makeup. Unlike my colored segregated school, in which most of the teachers held master's degrees, had extensive experience, and who held high expectations for student achievement; today, many African American students are taught by teachers, often among the least experienced, and who tend to hold lower expectations for African American students. This situation results in diminished expectations for these students' achievements and a departure from the strong focus on academic excellence that was a feature of the earlier colored segregated schools.

Despite unequal funding, poor facilities, and few resources, the environment of my colored schools provided the affective environment, institutional policies, and teacher excellence that enabled myself and others to achieve academically and experience success in the larger society.

The culture, climate, and curriculum of our colored segregated schools was informed by an empowerment pedagogy. Our teachers resisted and circumvented the caste education designed for us. While the larger society sent deprecating messages about colored people, our colored teachers and school provided a counter message. Unlike the experiences of many African American students today, our humanity was affirmed, heritage celebrated, and dignity restored.

The culture of colored segregated schools was grounded on beliefs about students and teacher roles/responsibilities. I have no idea of what low expectations could feel like in a school environment; we were believed to have unlimited potential, that all children could learn and succeed, and that one could always rise above one's current life condition.

Teaching was a mission rather than a job for my teachers, it was a means to uplift the race and demonstrate the community value of "giving back."

Teachers were responsible for student achievement by motivating and keeping students engaged. Teachers were obliged to hold the highest expectations for students, and never giving up on them.

The school climate in the segregated colored school was an outward expression and demonstration of the belief system espoused by teachers and administrators. Providing personal attention to students, to help them discover individual gifts and talents was key. Teachers probed to determine the cause of academic and other problems, and one of the most referred to interventions by colored teachers to raise the bar and set higher standards for student achievement was "pushing." Pushing was a teacher's demand that a student perform at a higher level than they thought they were capable. This colored girl became an essayist and won essays contests in high school because my English teacher, Mrs. Esther Dailey, "pushed me relentlessly."

The curriculum in my segregated colored school was expansive rather than contractive. Our teachers circumvented the prescribed caste education that would have prepared us for menial jobs and instead provided a liberal and college-preparatory education.

I am not naïve enough to believe that all segregated colored schools were as excellent as the ones I attended, however, if one takes a good look at the successes of the many leaders especially of the Civil Rights movement who attended these schools, then the empowering pedagogy described was the key to their success.

Over six decades after the Supreme Court declared "separate but equal" schools to be unconstitutional, today many schools remain highly segregated by race and ethnicity. Many African American students today are as disempowered by the educational system as I, a colored girl, was empowered. Equal educational opportunity remains an ideal rather than a reality for many African American students.

Person of the Global Majority

Cultural Adventures

Jaha and Martha
Kuala Lumpur, Malaysia

Martha and Cuban Friend Luis

Cultural Gathering

Since my birth more than seventy years ago, my human identity has been designated at all stages as inferior -- from colored to Negro, Black, African American, and even Person of Color to assign my place on the social/racial hierarchy of the United States. Despite federal laws, the narratives associated with my identity have never been equated with full "equality" in the nation. Each designation has separated my group from the privilege of simply being an American.

Language and narrative are powerful in designating a group's place in a society. Every designation assigned the African descendants of those enslaved in America has implied a negative identity, as in "lesser than" or the "other," and placed in negative relationship to whiteness, the standard of superiority.

Global Majority is a term which characterizes the collective ethnic groups which constitute approximately 85 percent of the global population. The term speaks to the centrality and power of language to liberate those groups that have through negative narratives been viewed as the other or inferior to whiteness. The term Global Majority does not situate whiteness as a reference point or superior status; persons becoming the Global Majority are no longer judged by the white norm. One's identity as a Person of the Global Majority does not exist in relation to whiteness and transcends one's geographic place of birth. It challenges the superiority of whiteness. Persons of the Global Majority have come from ancient and rich heritages that have contributed to world civilization since its beginnings.

It is the teachings and lessons from my days as a colored girl that have led me to the choice of identifying myself at this point in my life as a Person of the Global Majority. My attachment to this designation meets my human emotional needs of identity, belonging, and self-esteem.

- My sense of identity is enhanced through my cultural connections with the global majority. The collectivism of our cultures, cooperation, reciprocity, and interdependence, resulting in helping and sharing, and "giving back" are core values that I learned as a colored girl. The beliefs and values of my African ancestors are shared by this majority population of the globe. Our spiritual practices, reverence for ancestors, (from Mexico to Japan) are significant, our connection to harmony and respect for nature are the same.
- To be affiliated with and accepted by others in a society are crucial to one's sense of belonging. One of the most fulfilling times in my life was a visit to the Marshall Islands where I was invited to participate in a ritual with local chiefs to share sakau. I was totally accepted as one of our larger global society. As a colored girl, I was trained in having a good character so that I could relate to and respect all people. Also, visiting the home family of my son in Japan, the wife offered me a fork

for dinner, and her husband chastised her, telling her that I was a citizen of the world.
- My status and recognition derive from my descendance from ancestors who came to America from the three ancient West African kingdoms of Ghana, Mali, and Songhai. Knowing that my ancestors were deliberately chosen to be enslaved in the New World particularly because of their achievements in agriculture, architecture, and other disciplines fills me with pride.

My sense of self-definition, self-worth, and self-determination are fulfilled as I connect with those of my global culture. As a result, I will more fearlessly and strongly embrace my heritage and stay connected to the cultural practices that have sustained my people for almost four hundred years in this society. While I have never visited the continent of Africa, I have visited Cuba many times and was entranced and filled with the spirit of Africa and my global community there.

Conclusion

Matha and Bernice
Colored Girl

Martha - PGM

This colored girl and countless others like me created our own "place" in which we reached our full human potential. The knowledge of my true identity and my sense of worth provided the self-determination to use my unique gifts and talents to "give back" and uplift my community, to fulfill my life purpose, and to create the life I desired.

While racism has made me weep, consumed my ten-year-old mind with the vulnerability that no child should feel, and filled my heart with fear, the lessons learned from my family, community, and school have empowered me. I am forever grateful for the lessons learned as a colored girl. I was given the faith, hope, courage, and determination to be my true self, and to use my gifts for the betterment of all mankind.

Acknowledgements

My children, Jaha and Saba are my greatest achievement. I thank them for embracing the lessons and values I learned as a colored girl and passed on to them. I thank you Jaha for believing in me, taking on this project, and bringing Reflections to fruition as a book.

Thank you Amy Shumaker and Pamela James from WGCU for your belief in and support of Reflections. Thank you so much for getting the grant to make the documentary based on Reflections. Through your actions you are helping to "lift the veil".

I being an only child never had a biological sister but have gained several whom I love dearly over the years. Because of your love and sisterhood, I had the inspiration to write Reflections. Thank you my Delta Sigma Theta Soror and dear friend for over 60 years, Anitta Rutherford Orr; my Italian sister Norma Caltagirone who believed in me as a writer and had been a friend for over 40 years; my Jamaican sister, Clover Virgo who inspires me with her spiritual wisdom; my Irish sister Colleen O'Brien who is my muse and wonderful editor; and Angela Evans who watches over me constantly, lifts my spirit, and demands that I rest.

All of my sisters embody the values that have made them and myself whom we all are. In a sense we are all " colored " girls.

Love you all!!!
Martha

www.ingramcontent.com/pod-product-compliance
Lightning Source LLC
LaVergne TN
LVHW020133080526
838202LV00047B/3932